Winston Churchill

ROBERT BLAKE

SUTTON PUBLISHING

First published in 1998 by
Sutton Publishing Limited · Phoenix Mill
Thrupp · Stroud · Gloucestershire · GL5 2BU

Reprinted 2001

British Library Cataloguing in Publication Data

A catalogue record for this book is available from the British Library

ISBN 0 7509 1507 2

Typeset in 14/19.5pt Perpetua.
Typesetting and origination by
Sutton Publishing Limited.
Printed and bound in England by
J.H. Haynes & Co. Ltd, Sparkford.

Winston Churchill

Pocket BIOGRAPHIES

Series Editor C.S. Nicholls

Highly readable brief lives of those who have played a significant part in history, and whose contributions still influence contemporary culture.

CONTENTS

LIST OF PLATES

CHRONOLOGY

1874	**30 November**. Born at Blenheim Palace, Oxfordshire.
1886–94	Educated: Harrow and Sandhurst.
1895	Death of father, Lord Randolph. Joins 4th Hussars.
1896	Sent to India with his regiment.
1899	Defeated as Tory candidate in Oldham.
1899	Travels to South Africa as a war correspondent. Captured by the Boers.
1900	Stands again for Oldham in the general election and wins.
1906	Returned as a Liberal for North-West Manchester and becomes Under Secretary for the Colonies.
1908	**April.** Enters Cabinet as President, Board of Trade. **12 September**. Marries Clementine Hozier.
1909	Daughter Diana born.
1910–11	**January 1910 to October 1911**. Home Secretary under Asquith.
1911	Son Randolph born. Agadir Incident.

Chronology

1911	Becomes First Lord of the Admiralty.
1914	Daughter Sarah born.
	Crisis in Ireland over Home Rule.
	Outbreak of First World War.
1915	Dardanelles Campaign. Churchill removed from the Admiralty.
1917–19	Minister of Munitions under Lloyd George.
1918	Daughter Marigold born (dies in 1921).
1919–21	Secretary of State for War and Air.
1921–2	Secretary of State for Colonies and Air.
1922	Daughter Mary born.
	Chanak Incident, which leads to the fall of Lloyd George. Churchill loses his seat.
1924	Wins seat in Epping as a 'Constitutionalist' supported by the Conservative Association.
1924–9	Chancellor of the Exchequer.
1925	Returns to the Gold Standard.
1926	General Strike and National Gazette.
1931	Resigns from Shadow Cabinet over India.
1931–9	Political 'wilderness'. Warns against German rearmament.
1936	Churchill backs Edward VIII during the Abdication Crisis.
1939	War declared on Germany.
	Churchill becomes First Lord of the Admiralty again and member of the War Cabinet.

1940	Disastrous Norwegian Campaign; Government brought down.
	9 May. Churchill becomes Prime Minister.
1941	**December**. Pearl Harbour bombed. The USA enters the war.
1941–2	The Battle of the Atlantic.
1942	Fall of Singapore and Tobruk.
	Battle of El Alamein.
1943	Allied landings in North Africa and Italy.
	Italian surrender.
1944	The Normandy invasion.
	Moscow Conference.
1945	**February**. Yalta Conference.
	8 May. Germany surrenders.
	5 July. Crushing Conservative defeat in general election.
	Churchill resigns.
1946	'Iron Curtain' speech in Fulton, Missouri.
1951	Churchill becomes Prime Minister again.
1953	Survives serious illness concealed from the public.
1955	Churchill retires.
1965	**24 January**. Churchill dies.
	30 January. State funeral.

YOUTH AND ADVENTURE

Winston Leonard Spencer Churchill is generally regarded as one of Britain's greatest statesmen, ranking with the two Pitts, Peel, Gladstone and Lloyd George. But his reputation fluctuated violently during his lifetime. A distinguished historian, Sir Robert Rhodes James, tracing his career to 1939, could plausibly entitle his book *Churchill, A Study in Failure*. He was an object of blazing controversy from his youth onward. It was his role in war which established his fame, but this occurred only in the Second World War. His part in the First World or 'Great' War was a matter of bitter dispute at the time and still is. Nor have all his decisions during the Second World War gone unchallenged.

He was born prematurely in Blenheim Palace on 30 November 1874, the elder of two sons of Lord Randolph Churchill (younger son of the 7th Duke of Marlborough) and of Jennie Jerome, daughter of Leonard Jerome, a prominent and wealthy New York businessman. He was directly descended from the great Duke of Marlborough, who had no male heirs. The dukedom went by special remainder through the Duke's eldest daughter Anne, who had married Charles Spencer, Earl of Sutherland. It was not until 1817 that the family assumed the name of Churchill in addition to Spencer. The family had a bad reputation in society in the eighteenth and nineteenth centuries. They were dissolute and debt-ridden. By ducal standards they were far from wealthy (only £35,000 per annum) compared with Devonshire, Portland, Norfolk, Westminster and others. The expense of keeping up this style of life became increasingly irksome.

After a long line of mediocrities Lord Randolph was a throw-back to the earlier brilliance of the family. Like many younger sons within a heartbeat of grandeur, he was intensely ambitious. He was also very clever and had a command of language, which his son was to inherit. But he was reckless, extravagant and promiscuous. He had a bitter quarrel with the Prince of Wales at a time when royalty mattered politically. There were threats of a duel and his father the Duke accepted exile to Dublin as Viceroy of Ireland, taking his son as secretary to keep him out of mischief.

But he bounced back, entered Parliament for the family borough of Woodstock and, from 1880 onwards, headed a small group of Tory dissidents who in opposition made the life of their leader, Sir Stafford Northcote, almost as uncomfortable as that of the Prime Minister, Gladstone. Lord Randolph aimed high. But Lord Salisbury, the new leader of the party, was a very different proposition from Northcote. Back in office, he made Lord Randolph Chancellor of the Exchequer in 1886. The leadership seemed almost within his grasp. But he overreached himself by resigning in December on a trivial issue as a trial of strength. Lord Salisbury accepted at once. It was a classic case of rising like a rocket and falling like a stick. Salisbury repelled all efforts at reconciliation, observing that it would be odd for someone who had got rid of a carbuncle on his neck to want it back. Lord Randolph never held office again. His health rapidly declined. His speeches in the House became embarrassingly confused and incoherent. He died of tertiary syphilis at the beginning of 1895.

Winston Churchill had an unhappy childhood. His father, whom he loved and admired, was remote and cantankerous, given to outbursts of ill temper – possibly a symptom of his disease. His mother too was aloof and lacking in affection. His efforts to get either of them to turn up on parents' day occasions at his preparatory school or at Harrow nearly always failed. The one woman who gave him sympathy and love was his nurse, Mrs Everest, for whom he retained lasting affection till the day of her death when he was twenty, and whose funeral he tearfully attended. At Harrow, which he entered when he was twelve, the climate of the Hill being considered healthier than that of Eton, he made little mark. He was no good at Greek or Latin, the regular diet of public schools in those days, nor did he take to mathematics. But he did well in history and essay-writing. And he won a prize open to the whole school by reciting by heart the 1,200 lines of Macaulay's *Lays of Ancient Rome* without a single mistake. His diminutive height made it hard for him to flourish in games but did not prevent him winning the Public Schools Championship in fencing.

The Law, the Church and the Services were the obvious careers for an upper-class boy in those days. The first two presupposed an Oxford or Cambridge education, but this was ruled out by Churchill's weakness in classics. In any case, Lord Randolph regarded him as too stupid for the Bar, and, observing his son's passion for collecting toy soldiers – at the age of seven he had amassed over 1,000 – decided that the Army would be acceptable. The question was whether it would accept him. It did, but only on his third attempt, after leaving school and being taught by a 'crammer'. His affection for Harrow, however, was long-lasting and he attended its famous 'Songs' whenever he could, long into old age. His third attempt got him into Sandhurst as a cavalry cadet, a position easier to secure than one in the infantry but with the drawback of requiring a private income. This greatly annoyed Lord Randolph, who wrote a crushing letter of reproof instead of the congratulations that his son expected. But Churchill enjoyed Sandhurst and learned to ride well. 'No hour of life is lost', he wrote, 'that is spent in the saddle.'[1] He followed his father's political career with the keenest interest and often went to the Strangers' Gallery to hear him. But there was no rapport between them. 'When once I suggested that I might help his private secretary to write some of his letters, he froze me into stone.'[2] Lord Randolph died leaving a load of debts and an estranged wife, just before Winston joined his regiment, the 4th Hussars, early in 1895.

A young cavalry subaltern did not count for much in the world but an elder son of Lord Randolph Churchill did, especially when he was intensely ambitious, very clever and seldom lacking in effrontery. Churchill never regarded his military career as more than a launching pad for politics. So enlisting his hitherto aloof mother, he took full advantage of his grand connections. He sought as many campaign medals as he could get and resolved to use the power of his pen to make money. MPs were not paid in those days. An independent financial base was essential. The problem in the search for campaign medals was that there were scarcely any campaigns. The year 1895 was singularly peaceful. British troops were not engaged in fighting anywhere. This lull was not destined to last. Meanwhile, Churchill decided that, if he could not fight in a war he could at least watch one. A prolonged guerrilla campaign in Cuba between the libertarian rebels and the Spaniards who ruled the island as a colony was reaching its final stages. He obtained introductions from his father's friend Sir Henry Drummond Wolff, who was Ambassador in Madrid.

Cavalry officers in time of peace were entitled to a lavish total of five months' leave every year, including ten continuous weeks. The normal form was to spend the time fox-hunting. Churchill reckoned that a visit to Cuba as an observer would be more interesting and actually cheaper. The Commander-in-Chief, Lord Wolseley, gave permission slightly reluctantly. The rebel cause was popular in England, the Spanish government was not. Churchill and a fellow subaltern, Reginald Barnes, sailed for New York at the beginning of November. Churchill had made an arrangement with the *Daily Sketch* to send occasional letters from the Cuban Front for publication at £5 a time. His father had been paid £100 each for his letters from South Africa in 1891 but Churchill could hardly expect anything like that. It was his first foray into the journalism that was to be such a useful support for his style of life for much of his career.

The two young subalterns were courteously received in Havana and then joined a mobile column that had the double task of visiting the various townships and posts garrisoned by Spanish troops, and attacking the rebels wherever they could be found. On 30 November, his twenty-first birthday, Churchill had his baptism of fire in a brief skirmish early in the morning. No bullets seemed to come near him and he felt reassured, writing later 'I felt like the optimist "who did not mind what happened, so long as it did not happen to him" '.[3] After a few more days fighting the column returned to its base and Churchill and his companion sailed for home. He had sent five letters to the *Daily Sketch*. The publicity that attended his Cuban foray was far from favourable. In vain he denied having fired against the rebels on behalf of an odious tyranny, as the Radical Press saw it. The episode led to the myth that in 1898, when American forces intervened in Cuba, Churchill had fought on the 'wrong' side in the Spanish–American war. In fact, he was in India throughout the year and could not possibly have done anything of the sort.

In 1896 Churchill enjoyed for half a year the pleasures of the social round. 'I now passed', he wrote, 'a most agreeable six months; in fact they formed almost the only idle spell I have ever had.'[4] His account of it is vivid and compelling. The high point was the famous fancy dress ball at Devonshire House in 1897, which Churchill attended with his mother but this was when he was on leave from India to which his regiment had been posted, sailing from Southampton on 11 September 1896. He was far from enthusiastic at departing and tried hard to get himself attached to the 9th Lancers, who were going to Durban and thence to the war in Matabeleland (Zimbabwe). 'A few months in South Africa', he wrote to his mother, whom he was constantly importuning to pull strings, 'would earn me the SA medal and in all probability the [British South Africa] Company's star. Thence hot foot to Egypt – to return with two more decorations in a year or two.'[5] But his efforts were in vain and he tried to reconcile himself to the prospect of several years of tedious exile in India away from the centres of power and prestige.

Churchill's career in the sub-continent had an inauspicious start. While landing at Bombay from a small boat in a heavy swell he dislocated his shoulder. The matter did not seem serious at the time. 'I scrambled up all right, made a few remarks of a general character, mostly beginning with the earlier letters of the alphabet, hugged my shoulder and soon thought no more about it.'[6] In fact, the injury was to dog him all his life. He could never play tennis again, only play polo with one arm strapped to his side and endured repeated dislocations on inconvenient and unpredictable occasions.

India proved to be far less boring than he had feared. When and if time hung heavy on his hands he made it pass more quickly by a course in self-education. Lady Randolph sent him large book parcels. He read Gibbon, Macaulay and Lecky, and also Plato, Aristotle and

Schopenhauer in translation. He was greatly impressed by a now long-forgotten book, Winwood Reade's *The Martyrdom of Man* – 'a universal history of mankind, dealing in harsh terms with the mysteries of all religions and leading', as Churchill wrote in *My Early Life*, 'to the depressing conclusion that we simply go out like candles'.[7] Another favourite book was Bartlett's *Familiar Quotations*. 'It is a good thing', he wrote, 'for an uneducated man to read books of quotations.'[8]

There was also polo, at which he became adept despite his injury, to keep boredom at bay. Then while on leave in England he learned early in 1897 that a potential patron, Sir Bindon Blood, was to lead a punitive expedition against the rebellious Pathan tribes on the north-west frontier. Sir Bindon said there were no vacancies and he should come out as a war correspondent – which he did on behalf of the *Pioneer*, an important Indian newspaper, and the London *Daily Telegraph*. To his fury his letters in the latter were published unsigned. He soon found a place in the Malakand Field Force and took part in a ferocious campaign that nearly cost him his life. He made his experiences the basis of a book with the same title, written in great haste to forestall a similar work projected by a rival war correspondent, Lord Fincastle. Churchill won the race, but no one would read either book as a definitive account. Churchill was not interested in accuracy anyway – only in publicity. His next effort in that direction was a temporary posting to the Sudan, again as a war correspondent. Strings had to be pulled at the highest level. The commander of the force to avenge the death of General Gordon was Sir Herbert Kitchener. He regarded Churchill as a medal-hungry pusher whose despatches would be critical and damaging, as indeed they turned out to be. In 1898 Churchill took part at Omdurman in what is often – though wrongly – said to be the last cavalry charge in the history of the British Army. The episode is brilliantly described in *My Early Life*, and his Sudan experiences were the basis of Churchill's second book, *The River War* (1899).

Churchill's military career had almost ended. He returned briefly to India, where he was part of the winning team in the inter-regimental polo tournament. He began a novel, *Savrola*, which he temporarily put aside. In the autumn of 1899 the Boer War broke out and he got himself sent once more as a war correspondent, but no longer an Army officer, to South Africa, though he was far from welcome to Lord Roberts, the Commander-in-Chief, and even less so to Kitchener, Robert's Chief of Staff. As correspondent to the *Morning Post* he was paid £250 a month and all expenses – a very large figure for the time. He had by now resigned his commission and had stood as a Conservative candidate for Oldham in July. He lost narrowly. On 15 November, in the course of the South African war, he was taken prisoner while on an armoured train in Natal but escaped from Pretoria a month later, making his way after numerous vicissitudes by rail to Lourenço Marques (Maputo) and thence by boat to Durban, where he was given a hero's welcome.

The news spread all over the world. Like Byron he awoke to find himself famous, though for different reasons.

He was ready for a political career. He had the money for independence. From writing and lecturing he had made by 1900 some £10,000 — the equivalent of at least £400,000 in modern money, though such comparisons are always difficult. He had fallen in love with one Pamela Plowden in India, but nothing came of it. He was unattached as he embarked into the stormy sea of politics. He was somewhat worried when his mother, with whom he had had warm relations latterly, decided to marry someone twenty years younger. Her finances were as erratic as his had been until he struck oil as a writer and lecturer, and her new husband was not rich. Churchill could no longer depend on her to pull strings, but by now he hardly needed that help.

MEMBER OF PARLIAMENT

By 1900 Churchill, at twenty-six, was a well-known but by no means generally well-liked public figure. There were stories about his behaviour as a subaltern – rigging the result of a steeplechase challenge cup and bullying an unpopular brother officer, Alan Bruce, into resignation. A cloud hung over his escape from capture in South Africa – the charge that he broke his parole, also that he reneged on a pledge for a joint escape with two others and left them in the lurch. There is no truth in the escape allegations, though they dogged him for many years. The earlier charges have more substance. His son, Randolph, in his biography, writes, 'Neither the story of the Challenge Cup nor that of Bruce's reception into the Regiment reads very prettily,' but concludes that 'although Churchill's conduct may have been injudicious it was in no way dishonourable'.[1] Not everyone took this charitable view.

'With words we govern man,' Disraeli once said. Churchill was a master of words and took immense trouble over his writing, his speeches and lectures. His style with its overtones of Gibbon, and Macaulay (whom he later came to hate), commanded attention and produced money. He could now confidently seek a seat. He left South Africa in 1900 and stood for Parliament, again for Oldham, in the general election of that year. The tide was flowing for the Conservatives and he got in but his views about his party soon became increasingly disenchanted. An element in this change may have been his undertaking to write a life of his father. On reading the documents, he came to believe that Lord Randolph had been badly treated by the Tory establishment. But there were other reasons for his subsequent decision to move to the Liberals – above all his grave doubts about the policy of tariff reform that was sweeping the party under the influence of Joseph Chamberlain.

Meanwhile, he made, characteristically ignoring tradition, a contentious maiden speech, praising the Boers. *'If I were a Boer'*, he said, *'I hope I should be fighting in the field.'*[2] He caused great offence to the Conservatives and continued to do so on many other issues, including a fierce and well-argued attack on expenditure on armaments – the issue on which his father had resigned in 1886. In 1903, when the split between Conservative free traders and tariff reformers had become ruinously divisive, he proclaimed himself 'an Independent Conservative'. In the landslide election of 1906 he stood as a declared Liberal and was returned for North-West Manchester with a large majority.

His reward was office as Under-Secretary for the Colonies. His chief was in the Lords, so Churchill had the task of dealing with the

Commons which of course he greatly welcomed. The colonies meant Africa and Churchill was well qualified by his experience to cope with the problems of British rule. His main task was to prepare a new constitution for South Africa, an arrangement for 'responsible government'. He wanted it to be a matter of all-party support, 'a gift of England'. Edward VII congratulated him on putting country before party. Churchill made another visit to South Africa in the autumn of 1907, which produced another book, *My African Journey*. His energy and assiduity were immense. He never relaxed. He had a finger in every pie within his reach. But he combined these qualities with an insensitivity to the feelings of others which lasted for the whole of his long life.

A striking example was his first front-bench speech in 1906. It was a 'defence' of Lord Milner, Britain's pro-consul in South Africa during and after the Boer War. Milner was charged with authorizing illegal floggings of imported Chinese labourers in the mines. Churchill's was the sort of defence that any defendant could happily do without. Condescending, patronizing and arrogant his speech caused enormous offence. Milner was a Conservative icon, but even the dominant Liberals were embarrassed. Churchill had many virtues but tact was not one of them. He was much involved in the grant of self-government to the Transvaal and the Orange Free State. Cape Town and Natal already had it, and the ultimate result was the Union of South Africa in 1910. Churchill's hope that a liberal-minded English-speaking electorate would take the lead was over-optimistic but he could hardly have been expected to foresee *apartheid*.

By the time of the Act of Union Churchill had moved on and up. The new Prime Minister, H.H. Asquith, reconstructed his government after the resignation and death in April 1908 of his predecessor, Campbell-Bannerman. He appointed Lloyd George as his successor to the Exchequer and Churchill as President of the Board of Trade with a seat in the Cabinet. He was only thirty-three. He and Lloyd George were to be formidable allies in laying the foundations of what came later to be known as the Welfare State. He was now loathed by most Conservatives. 'Rats' are always hated by the party they have deserted – the more so when they attack it in language as intemperate and colourful as he employed. Great was the glee of his enemies when he lost his seat in the by-election that, under the rules of the day, had to be fought by a member who accepted a new office. It was a blow but he soon got back for Dundee, a safe working-class seat.

The same year (1908) that saw Churchill's entry into the Cabinet also saw his marriage. His father had been not only a philanderer but an explorer of the shady side of Victorian sexual practices. There is no evidence to suggest that Churchill engaged in these activities. Indeed, if he knew the nature of Lord Randolph's illness he would not have risked, morality apart, the red light districts of London or India. His name had been vaguely linked with various reputable girls but in a platonic and somewhat lukewarm way. One of these had been Clementine Hozier, whom he met at a ball in Crewe House in the spring of 1904, but they did not 'hit it off'. She regarded him as gauche, awkward and discourteous. He did not offer to dance with her or take her in to supper. He had then as always no gift of 'small talk'. Four years later they met at a dinner party given by her aunt, Lady Helier. Churchill nearly cut the party, only persuaded by his faithful aid, Edward Marsh, that it was his duty to turn up. Clementine too was a reluctant guest. But it turned out to be a case of love at second sight. Five months later, on 11 August at Blenheim, they were driven to seek refuge from a rainstorm in the ornamental temple of Diana. He proposed and was accepted. They were married at St Margaret's Westminster on 12 September. Lord Hugh Cecil was best man and Lloyd George, chatting loudly with the bridegroom about politics, signed the register.

The pair were truly in love but Churchill's words in *My Early Life* that they lived happily ever after must be taken with several pinches of salt. Clementine was ten years younger and, although there is no hint of marital infidelity on either side, their styles of life were very different. At an early stage they slept in separate bedrooms – a not unusual feature of Edwardian married life. He liked breakfast in bed and, although he awoke early, he got up late after spending the morning writing and reading. After lunch he would take a catnap and thus fortified would work and talk either in the House of Commons or at home till the small hours. She got up early and retired early. There were stormy scenes. She deeply disapproved of some of his more raffish friends, F.E. Smith, Lord Beaverbrook and later Brendan Bracken. She was irritated by his habit of bringing unexpected guests to impromptu dinner parties. She disapproved of his love of drink and gambling, and was to be greatly distressed when he bought Chartwell without consulting her and at a cost which far exceeded their means.

Her mother, Lady Blanche Hozier, a daughter of the Earl of Airlie, had for years lived apart from her nominal father, Sir Henry. Her real father was generally believed to be one of Lady Blanche's numerous lovers, Captain 'Bay' Middleton. Clementine was a strong Liberal. She was unhappy when Churchill went back to the Conservatives in 1924. She urged him not to accept the party leadership in 1940, and when after 1965 she was made a life Baroness as a posthumous gesture to Churchill she sat on the cross benches and not among the Conservatives. Their somewhat turbulent marriage produced five children, one of whom died in childhood. Three daughters and a son survived – Randolph, Sarah, Diana and Mary, the youngest, who married Christopher Soames.

The Board of Trade dealt with many of the functions subsequently assigned to the Ministry of Labour employment – working hours, labour exchanges, wage levels, trade unions, strikes and conciliation. Churchill was not good at conciliation. He listened too little and talked too much. But he made a good deal of headway in matters such as 'sweated labour' and Trade

Boards – 'wages councils' as they were later called. More importantly, as a member of the Cabinet he could have a say in general policy well beyond his ministerial remit. Bills about shipping, electricity and insurance were not all that important, but the Cabinet's struggles about rearmament and the budget were crucial and affected the course of history. At this stage of his career, Churchill shared his father's doubts about defence expenditure. He believed that it was not enough to sustain a major military role in Europe, which he regarded as unnecessary anyway. And he thought it was too much, indeed extravagant, for the defence of the overseas empire. The money saved could be used for the social reforms that Lloyd George and he supported. The crunch came in 1909. Three years earlier Britain had produced the first 'Dreadnought', with a speed and all-round armament of heavy guns that made all previous battleships obsolete. The German Navy at once followed suit. The naval race had begun. In December 1908 Reginald McKenna, First Lord of the Admiralty, pressed that Britain should lay down six of the new warships instead of four as originally planned. This was a blow to the Lloyd George/Churchill plans for social reform and they fiercely opposed it. Eventually there was a compromise. Four would be laid down at once and another four if later evidence showed this to be essential. Naturally the naval authorities argued that it did, and carried the Cabinet. So the 'compromise' between four and six resulted in eight, egged on by the popular slogan, 'We want eight and we won't wait'.

Defeated by the naval lobby, Lloyd George and Churchill were not going to be baulked of their social reform objectives. The Budget of 1909 contained some highly controversial and, by the standards of the day, swingeing tax increases. In order to pay for unemployment and health insurance, and for non-contributory old age pensions, income tax went up from 12 to 14 pence in the pound, death duties were doubled, a 'super tax' on the incomes of the very rich was introduced, and – the last straw for infuriated Tories — a wealth tax of 20 per cent was to be levied on the unearned increment on land values. It proved to be totally impracticable and was never in the end collected, but the threat was a red rag to the angry landowners who dominated the House of Lords. It resulted in the crowning Tory folly of using the Upper House to reject the Budget — contrary to all parliamentary precedent. The upshot was a major constitutional crisis, two general elections in 1910, which left the Liberals in office but with a much reduced majority dependent on the Irish Nationalist Members, and the reduction of the power of the Lords to one of delay instead of veto. The Parliament Act of 1911 that did this was only carried amid scenes of apoplectic rage by the threat to swamp the Lords with new creations.

During this crisis Churchill was on his most provocative form. It is hard to exaggerate the hatred with which he was regarded by his former colleagues.

After the first election in 1910 Asquith

reconstructed his Cabinet. He offered Churchill the Irish Secretaryship. Churchill prudently refused to lie on this bed of nails and asked for the Admiralty or the Home Office. The latter only was vacant, its previous incumbent having accepted the office of Governor-General of South Africa. So Churchill went to the Home Office – one of the three great offices of state after the premiership – at the age of thirty-five. It involved a curious miscellany of topics. He found himself answering questions in the Commons on such diverse matters as the censorship of plays, the conditions for the immigration of Italian ice-cream vendors and the regulations governing the mudguards of motor cars. He also had the task, formerly carried out by the Prime Minister, of writing a long-hand account to the King of proceedings in the Commons. His tenure was less than two years, January 1910 to October 1911. His knack of living in a blaze of publicity had not deserted him. There was the matter of miners on strike in the Rhondda Valley, who rioted in the town of

Tonypandy and wrecked numerous shops. Troops were ordered to go there by the GOC of Southern Command without Home Office authority. Churchill decided to keep them in reserve and send a detachment of Metropolitan Police to support the local force; the riots were suppressed without loss of life and no troops were involved. But Churchill had told the Miners' Federation that he would not hesitate to invoke the Army if there was no other way of preserving order. The fact that he did not need to do so was soon submerged in the myth of military intervention. The cry of 'Tonypandy' was raised again and again at public meetings.

Then there was the 'Battle of Sidney Street'. Churchill was photographed when he seemed to be commanding personally a military force to crush a gang of anarchists who had killed three policemen and had holed up in a house in the vicinity. Soldiers were authorized by Churchill to assist the police. An exchange of shots occurred and the house caught fire. Churchill supported the officer in charge, who refused to allow the fire brigade to extinguish it. Two charred bodies were found in the embers.

There were other episodes in 1910 and 1911 (a period of acute labour unrest) when Churchill seemed, however unfairly, to be trigger-happy. One of the worst of these was the railway strike of 1911. It was an issue on which, unlike Tonypandy, he displayed reckless disregard of the rules about the relations normally respected between the civil and military authorities. He was for ever after detested by organized labour.

THREE

ADMIRALTY
1911–15

In the summer of 1911 an international crisis occurred that was to transform Churchill's career. The German government sent a gunboat, the *Panther*, to the port of Agadir on the Atlantic coast of Morocco. This was a riposte to the sending by France of an expeditionary force to Fez supposedly to protect European citizens in the capital who, it was claimed, were endangered by a rebellion against the Sultan of Morocco. The Germans believed that the real motive was to repeat in Morocco what France had already done in Tunis; occupation of Agadir would give Germany leverage to secure 'compensation' elsewhere. War seemed a real possibility. In a famous speech at the Mansion House on 21 July, Lloyd George made it clear that Britain would stand by France. Coming from the leader of the pacifist wing of the Liberals and the man most anxious for an Anglo-German accord, this caused a great sensation. The crisis blew over, the *Panther* departed from Agadir and Germany was 'compensated' on the Congo. But in retrospect the episode can be seen as the first of many stages in the process that culminated in the First World War.

A by-product of the incident was a major British reassessment of the roles of the Army and Navy in the event of hostilities with Germany. At a crucial meeting of the Committee of Imperial Defence convened by Asquith on 23 August, it became clear that the War Office, with the advantage of the military general staff initiated by the War Secretary Haldane after 1905, was far better prepared and had much clearer ideas than the Admiralty. Asquith became convinced that the Navy needed a war staff too. The First Lord, McKenna, had done much but on this point he had made no headway against the naval hierarchy. The obvious move was to make Haldane First Lord but he had recently accepted a peerage and it was essential that a reforming political head of the senior service should be answerable to the Commons. Failing Haldane, the politician most likely to infuse new life into the Admiralty was Churchill. Accordingly Asquith made a swap between him and McKenna, much to the latter's chagrin. On 25 October 1911 Churchill became First Lord.

Formally, this was not promotion. In the Cabinet pecking order the First Lord ranked below the Chancellor of the Exchequer and the Home and Foreign Secretaries. It was nonetheless a key post, far more important than the Home Office, given the gathering clouds of a war that, if it came, could only be with Germany. And Germany was doing all it could in the naval race to catch up with Britain, whose survival depended entirely on its Navy. Churchill adored his new position and was never happier than during the years till May 1915 while he held the office. His dismissal was the greatest political blow that he ever sustained, even greater than the loss of the 1945 election.

He inherited a Navy riven by furious feuds. The vendetta carried on by Admiral 'Jackie' (later Lord) Fisher with Admiral Lord Charles Beresford was a notorious and damaging scandal. By 1911 the two deadly rivals had reluctantly retired, but repercussions reverberated. The inhabitants of the 'Fish Pond' were hated by the Beresfordians. Churchill first met Fisher in 1907 and was at once fascinated by his picturesque and iconoclastic language, rather like Churchill's own. Both were anti 'establishment' men, essentially radical enemies of stuffy conservatism. Churchill contemplated bringing Fisher back as First Sea Lord. He was to do this with dire consequences in 1914 but caution at this time prevailed for once. He decided to use Fisher as a private adviser.

Churchill had been a leading supporter, along with Lloyd George, of cutting defence expenditure. He now swung to the opposite extreme. He always supported with fanatical energy the interests of whatever department of state he headed. He plunged into detail and spent more time in the Admiralty yacht, *Enchantress*, than any First Lord ever before or since. But, as someone wrote, a minister who insists on inspecting the bottom of every mine is liable to emerge with tunnel vision. Churchill's temperament had an obsessional side through-out his life and he never got rid of the itch to interfere in matters of detail.

He presided over many reforms. The conditions, barbarous and insanitary, of the lower deck were improved and pay raised. The education and recruitment of cadets were rationalized and up-dated. The most important change of all to which Churchill contributed was from coal-firing to oil-firing. The difference both to efficiency and the life-style of the crew can scarcely be exaggerated. Churchill also made some progress, if not quite enough, towards a naval staff. Another contribution was to encourage the naval air arm, for which object with his usual energy he decided to learn to fly

personally – to the consternation of his advisers
and family. His most notable achievement as
First Lord was to have the Fleet in complete
readiness to take its appropriate positions if and
when war broke out with Germany. He could
not have done this without the support and
advice of a host of able naval officers, some of
whom on occasions dissuaded him from plans
which might have been disastrous – for
example, the 'close blockade' of the German
coast and harbours. But he could take pride in
the fact that when hostilities began every ship
was at its allotted station.

Meanwhile, he had been involved in one of
the most controversial episodes in his career.
The general elections of 1910 gave the balance
of power in the Commons to the eighty Irish
Nationalist Members led by John Redmond. The
Liberal government now had to do something
about Irish Home Rule or else face defeat. The
Conservatives had always detested the notion of
a Dublin parliament and they no longer had the
barrier of the House of Lords to stop it. The

measure proposed in 1912 would be enacted after two years whatever the peers said or did. On the face of things a limited degree of self-government seemed not unreasonable. It had successfully been granted in Australia, New Zealand, Canada and recently in South Africa. But the position in Ireland was not the same. Ireland was – and is – an island containing two nations, a Roman Catholic majority and a Protestant minority divided by centuries of bitter hatred and mistrust. The cause of the Ulster Protestants had been sustained in unforgettable language by Churchill's father. 'Ulster will fight and Ulster will be right.'

And by 1912 fight was just what looked like happening. The previous year Edward Carson, leader of the Ulster Unionists, had announced plans to set up a provisional government to take charge of the Province of Ulster as soon as the Home Rule Bill was enacted. Men began to learn military drill, and early in 1913 an Ulster Volunteer Force was formed to resist by arms if necessary the imposition of rule from Dublin.

The argument was that if the Catholic Irish of the south had a moral claim to choose how they were governed, so too had the Protestants of the north. Churchill, conscious that his father's attitude was anathema to the Liberals, had hitherto kept clear of Irish affairs. But he was aware that his own credit with the party was none too good in view of his change of course over naval rearmament. To take a firm line with the Ulster movement would help to restore his position. He did not lack sympathy with Ulster but he always believed that the threat of force should be met by force. When the threat had been defeated, then was the time for compromise.

The situation was made no easier by a change in the leadership of the Tory Party, which was to have a baleful effect on Churchill's career. In November 1911 Bonar Law succeeded Balfour. He came from a very different world. A dour Glaswegian businessman of Ulster ancestry and born in New Brunswick, he talked 'another language' and he deeply distrusted Churchill from the beginning. Early in 1914 it looked as if the Army itself would not support Home Rule. Much has been written about the so-called 'mutiny' of the Curragh, the main Army base near Dublin. It was not a 'mutiny'. Officers were given a choice by the War Office to resign if they were not willing to enforce Home Rule on Ulster. A large number chose to resign. It seemed a revolutionary situation. Churchill as First Lord ordered the Third Battle Squadron stationed on the Atlantic coast of France to move to Lamlash near Arran, only 70 miles from Belfast. If there was armed resistance to Home Rule he could, he said, have Belfast in ruins in twenty-four hours. Balfour described him as 'an agent provocateur'. The Irish crisis died – for the moment only – with the outbreak of war in 1914, but Conservative hatred of Churchill knew no bounds.

When Germany invaded Belgium on 4 August 1914 Churchill was the leading figure in a divided Cabinet to support armed intervention. He had already on his own authority mobilized the Fleet three days earlier when news came through of the German declaration of war on Russia. His notable achievement over Belgium was to persuade Lloyd George to back an ultimatum to Germany. In the end, only two ministers resigned.

For the next nine months Churchill was in his element at the Admiralty, taking a large personal part in many decisions that his critics believed to be the remit of the Sea Lords. The First Sea Lord was Prince Louis of Battenberg whose German origins caused him to resign as the result of a wave of xenophobia. Churchill long felt guilty at not having supported him more strongly – which may explain the over-promotion of the Prince's son, Lord Louis Mountbatten, in the Second World War. In Battenberg's place Churchill brought back Lord Fisher. It was a disastrous decision. There was no room for two prima donnas in this opera, especially as one of them was an impetuous and egotistic 74-year-old.

The naval war did not run smoothly. The German warships *Goeben* and *Breslau* escaped through the eastern Mediterranean into Turkish territorial waters, owing to ambiguous signals from the Admiralty War Staff to the Admiral commanding the Mediterranean fleet. The two ships played an important part in bringing Turkey into war on the German side a few weeks later. Success in the North Sea at the battle of Heligoland Bight was balanced by the sinking of three old armoured cruisers near the Dutch coast. Errors by the naval staff were largely responsible for the annihilation on 2 November of Admiral Cradock's South American Squadron at Coronel on the coast of Chile. This disaster was only in part redeemed by the destruction of the German squadron a few weeks later at the Falkland Islands. Churchill's reputation was further damaged by his ill-fated efforts to save Antwerp in October 1914. He went there himself and offered to take personal command of the forces involved – an offer rejected by the Cabinet amid much merriment. The Antwerp expedition may have held up the German advance into northern

France and, as Churchill argued, saved Dunkirk and Calais. But Antwerp fell with a loss of 2,500 men killed, wounded or interned, and Churchill was blamed.

The Antwerp affair had done Churchill no good. It was followed early in 1915 by an episode with which his name was to be forever associated and which damaged him much more seriously than Antwerp. The Dardanelles Campaign was an almost unmitigated disaster and, although plenty of others had responsibility, including both the Prime Minister (Asquith) and the Secretary for War (Kitchener), the idea was largely Churchill's and there can be little doubt that but for his unrelenting pressure, it would never have been undertaken. The purpose was to escape from the trench war stalemate on the Western Front, knock Turkey out of the war, supply arms through the Black Sea to Russia and thus bring renewed pressure on Germany's eastern front. In the great divide over strategy between 'easterners' and 'westerners', Churchill was a convinced easterner. The literature on the Dardanelles is enormous, and much of it highly tendentious, not least Churchill's own account in *The World Crisis* which is anything but reliable. A major error was his belief, contrary to his own conviction only three years earlier, that the assault could be achieved by naval bombardment alone. This was attempted early in 1915 and was a total failure. Churchill had misled himself by drawing a false lesson from the German successes on land against the allegedly impregnable forts in the Low Countries. The circumstances were entirely different and irrelevant. It was agreed by the Cabinet that naval operations were not enough and that a major military landing in Gallipoli was imperative. Thenceforth Churchill's responsibility was shared by Kitchener. The military story was of one disaster after another.

During all this time Fisher became ever more uneasy about his own position as First Sea Lord and his doubts mounted about the strategy of Churchill who, as throughout his life, was singularly insensitive to the feelings of others. Churchill himself later described the Army landings as a legitimate war gamble. By early May it was clear that the gamble had not come off. Fisher's silent but long-held misgivings came to a head. He resigned on 15 May and went into hiding. The sensation was immense. Combined with the totally separate matter of the shell shortage on the Western Front, it ended the uneasy parliamentary truce between Asquith and Bonar Law. The Prime Minister felt obliged to invite the Conservatives to join in a coalition. Bonar Law, who had always been anti-Dardanelles, made it a firm condition that Churchill should leave the Admiralty and was unmoved by his frantic pleas to stay.

Asquith regarded Bonar Law with some contempt but he had no option if the coalition was to get off the ground; Churchill could not remain at the Admiralty. He was lucky to remain in the government at all, bitterly and unfairly grumbling at Asquith's alleged weakness. His dismissal was the first major setback in a career so far of great success. But he was only forty and there was plenty of time for recovery.

FOUR

RECOVERY AND RELAPSE 1915–39

Churchill lingered on in government for a few more months in the sinecure office of Chancellor of the Duchy of Lancaster. He who had moved warships from ocean to ocean now had little more to do than sign the commission of new justices of the peace in Bootle. He was still a member of the Dardanelles Committee but he had no real say in policy. When it was reconstructed as the smaller War Committee he was excluded. On 15 November he resigned to serve for six months as a battalion commander on the Western Front. Meanwhile, to his consternation, the government, undeterred by prophecies of doom and gloom, decided to evacuate Gallipoli. The withdrawal accomplished without a single casualty was about the only success in the dreadful Dardanelles Campaign. It owed nothing to Churchill.

His decision to go on active service in the Army made a good public impression. He soon blotted it by returning briefly to Westminster in March 1916 to make an attack on the government – by now he hated Asquith – in the course of which he made the insane proposal that Fisher should be brought back to the Admiralty. It was received with ridicule. His friends were in despair. He was reluctantly persuaded to go back to France.

In the summer of 1916 he decided to return to politics. But he was now an outsider. Most of his time for the rest of the year was spent in giving evidence to the commission appointed to investigate the Gallipoli fiasco. Its first report came out in 1917. To some extent it exonerated Churchill but by no means entirely.

He played little part in the complicated intrigues that resulted in the fall of Asquith in December 1916 and his replacement by Lloyd George. He was bitterly disappointed at not being given office. As in 1915 Bonar Law and other major Tory figures made his exclusion an absolute condition of their joining the new coalition.

But six months later in 1917 the Prime Minister felt strong enough to bring him back — perhaps on Lyndon Johnson's principle that it is better to have someone who pisses out of your tent than into it. There was also the matter of Liberal representation. Asquith and most of the old guard stood aloof from Lloyd George, whose government was dominated by Conservatives. Churchill would redress the balance. Lloyd George, without consulting Bonar Law, made him Minister of Munitions. The Conservatives, including their leader, were furious. The Tory press was outraged. The *Morning Post* wrote, 'Although we have not yet invented the unsinkable ship we have discovered the unsinkable politician. . . . We confidently anticipate that he will continue to make colossal blunders at the cost of the nation.'[1] Lloyd George admitted in his memoirs that the government's life was threatened, but Bonar Law, however much he disliked Churchill, defended the Prime Minister's right of choice, and the row gradually died away – the process helped by the Prime Minister's guarantee that Churchill would have no say in war strategy or tactics; he was not a member of the smaller Inner Cabinet invented by Lloyd George after the fall of Asquith. Churchill was not consulted – or not overtly – on the key decisions of 1917–18. Confined to his department, he was energetic and vigorous. Inheriting a collection of competing, back-biting, separate organizations housed in different places all over London, he managed to centralize and rationalize a chaotic system, reducing fifty sub-departments to ten and establishing an inner council to run the Ministry's affairs. Although Churchill was not supposed to take part in war strategy, his restless energy as he whizzed to and from the Western Front inspired much suspicion. In terms of practical policy he concentrated on four 'new' arms – planes, tanks, gas and

Blenheim Palace, Oxfordshire, where Churchill was born in 1874. (Aerofilms)

Lady Randolph Churchill with her two sons, Jack and Winston, 1889. (Hulton Getty Images)

Churchill during the Boer War, *c.* 1900. (Picture from Churchill College: reproduced with permission of Curtis Brown Ltd, London, on behalf of Winston S. Churchill. The Broadwater collection)

Churchill watches (the left of the two men in top hats) as the military go into action at the Sidney Street siege, January 1911. At this time, he was Home Secretary. (Hulton Getty Images)

Churchill speaking at the 1908 by-election in North-West Manchester, in which he was beaten. Immediately afterwards he was elected for Dundee, which he represented until 1922. (Popperfoto)

Churchill with Edward Marsh, his devoted secretary who served him in every government office he held between 1905 and 1929. (Picture from Churchill College: reproduced with permission of Curtis Brown Ltd, London, on behalf of Winston S. Churchill. The Broadwater collection)

Churchill, in a photograph published in *Tatler*, just before the outbreak of the First World War, 1914, while he was serving as First Lord of the Admiralty. His wife, Clementine, is shown in the inset. (Picture from Churchill College: reproduced with permission of Curtis Brown Ltd, London, on behalf of Winston S. Churchill. The Broadwater collection)

Churchill with F.E. Smith.
(Churchill College)

Inspecting war damage in London, 8 September 1940. (Imperial War Museum, H3977)

Churchill and Roosevelt at the Casablanca Conference, 1943. (*Illustrated London News*)

Churchill in the field with Lt-Gen G.G. Simonds, Gen Sir B. Montgomery, and Lt-Gen Sir M.C. Dempsey, *c.* 1944. (Imperial War Museum, B7879)

Churchill with Roosevelt and Stalin at the Yalta Conference in February 1945.
(*Illustrated London News*)

The VE Day broadcast, 8 May 1945. (Imperial War Museum, H41845)

Churchill, *c.* 1940, in the now
famous stance. (*Illustrated
London News*)

Churchill died on 24 January
1965, at the age of ninety. His
state funeral took place on
30 January 1965. Here,
Clementine and Randolph
Churchill follow his coffin down
the steps of St Paul's Cathedral.
(Churchill College)

machine-guns — but he underestimated the difficulties of production and often got his figures wrong. Yet no one can doubt that as always he galvanized the Ministry that he headed.

After the Armistice of 1918 Lloyd George's coalition won a crushing victory. He reverted to the normal peacetime Cabinet in November 1919. Till then Churchill, though moved to the post of Secretary for War and Air, remained in the outer ring. His attempt to become Minister of Defence with control over the Admiralty as well and a seat in the Inner Cabinet was rebuffed by Lloyd George. Much of his work during 1919–20 concerned the highly controversial problems of demobilization. He was also involved in the matter of extricating the British forces stranded in Russia after the Bolsheviks had made a separate peace with Germany at Brest-Litovsk early in 1918. Churchill regarded the Bolsheviks as quintessentially evil. Just as Burke predicted that the French Revolution would be the prelude to tyranny in the name of 'the people', so Churchill foresaw Bolshevism as the destruction of all liberty. He thought that the evacuation of British forces from Russia could be turned round into an operation to topple Lenin and Trotsky. Lloyd George did not agree and applied his veto. The troops were evacuated; the Bolsheviks remained in power and were to stay for another seventy years. Churchill, deeply frustrated, never lost his loathing for the regime. His alliance with Stalin in 1941 was tactical only. Afterwards in 1949 he said, 'The strangling of Bolshevism at its birth would have been an untold blessing to the human race'. In 1919–20 his well-publicized fear of the Bolshevik threat merely confirmed his image as a warmonger, which was to be enhanced by the Chanak Incident two years later.

Meanwhile, Lloyd George, perhaps influenced by a desire to avoid trouble, shunted him at the end of February 1921 into the Colonial Office where he was charged with doing something to tidy up the legacy in the Middle East bequeathed by the collapse of the Ottoman Empire. He did

what he could to solve insoluble problems –
Iraq, Palestine, Transjordan; they still remain
unsolved today.

Churchill was less and less at ease with Lloyd
George, whose long reign, he saw, would soon
be over. He was moving to the right and
strongly supported the 'Black and Tans' in their
repression of Irish rebels responding to terror
with terror. He was on the Sinn Fein kidnap list
for a time and felt it wise to sleep, revolver at
the ready, in a steel protected attic rather than
his normal bedroom. In the end, mutual
exhaustion produced a compromise between the
rebels and the government – the famous 'treaty'
of partition. Churchill was closely involved in
the negotiations which have been a matter of
heated controversy ever since.

His last major crisis as Colonial Secretary was
the Chanak Incident in 1922. The Turks under
new leadership repudiated that part of the
Versailles settlement, known as the Treaty of
Sèvres, which gave large slices of the Turkish
coast to Greece. A Turkish nationalist army led

by Mustapha Kemal drove the Greeks out and threatened to cross the Dardanelles where there was a small British defence force in Chanak. The Cabinet saw this as a *casus belli*. Churchill tried with limited success to enlist the Dominion governments. They were annoyed to read his plea in the newspapers before they had had time to decipher the confidential telegrams. Only New Zealand expressed support. In the end, thanks to the good sense of the Army commander on the spot, who applied the Nelsonian blind eye to his orders, war was averted but Churchill's reputation for belligerency remained.

Chanak brought down the uneasy Lloyd George coalition. The Tory back-benchers had had enough. At a meeting in the Carlton Club in October 1922 they ousted their leader, Austen Chamberlain. He was succeeded by a reluctant Bonar Law, who became Prime Minister and won the ensuing general election in which Churchill, laid low by appendicitis, lost his seat. He did not get back into the Commons till the election of 1924, having contested without success two by-elections, one under Liberal colours, the second as an Independent Anti-Socialist in March 1924. He had repudiated the Liberals because of their decision to put Labour into office in the 'hung parliament' produced by the 1923 general election. Labour was committed to the recognition of Bolshevik Russia – to Churchill an unforgivable sin. The third general election in two years occurred after the fall of Ramsay MacDonald in October. Churchill stood for Epping as a 'Constitutionalist' with the support of the local Conservative Association. Third time lucky he won easily in a nationwide Conservative landslide.

His enforced leisure during 1922–4 had been largely occupied by writing a history of the First World War. Balfour observed, 'Winston has written a book about himself and called it *The World Crisis*'. It is not so much history as the material for historians. It is, as Churchill himself said of the volumes he wrote about the Second World War, 'my case'. It is wonderfully readable and made him a great deal of money.

But with election victory, he now had to lay aside authorship. He expected office but not the one he got. Baldwin made him, after Neville Chamberlain had refused, Chancellor of the Exchequer. It was a bizarre appointment and astonished the political world. Churchill's experience in office was no preparation for this post and he knew very little about finance or economics. His first problem was whether to bring Britain back to the Gold Standard at its pre-war dollar parity of $4.86. Strongly pressed by the entire financial establishment he agreed, though much worried by the deflationary effect on exports and employment of which he was warned by Keynes. His doubts were right. The decision led to the miners' strike and then to the General Strike of 1926. Churchill was hyperactive in its defeat, editing the *British Gazette* as a substitute for strike-bound Fleet Street papers. But the ultimate responsibility for crushing the strikers lay with Stanley Baldwin and the Cabinet, though Churchill's part was prominent and neither forgotten nor forgiven by the unions. His name was to be anathema to organized Labour for many years to come.

Churchill was not a radical or innovative Chancellor. His five budgets, 1924–9, did little that any other Chancellor would not have done. His strong opposition to rearmament was a factor in the very weakness of British defence, which he was to criticize so severely in the 1930s.

The Conservatives were marginally defeated in 1929. Ramsay MacDonald became Prime Minister, head of a Labour government till the economic crisis of 1931, and of a Conservative-dominated coalition government after Labour's crushing defeat that year. He remained in power till 1935 when Baldwin, the long-standing 'mayor of the palace', succeeded him. Churchill was not included by either MacDonald or Baldwin.

He was not unduly disturbed by loss of office in 1929 and set off with his brother and his son Randolph on an enjoyable tour of Canada and the United States. Back in England, restless and frustrated, though busily writing, he took up a new cause that was to be politically disastrous and keep him out of office for ten 'wilderness years'. This was India. He bitterly objected to Baldwin's agreement to support a bi-partisan policy of limited self-government. He used every trick of parliamentary procedure to block it. He had the support of a die-hard right-wing group of Tory MPs, but the vast majority supported the MacDonald–Baldwin partnership as did the rump of the Labour Party. He failed and did himself much harm in the process; he ruled himself out of office for a decade. In the Commons he had become something of a bore. This was unfortunate, for the next cause that he took up was, unlike India, one that really mattered – the rising threat of Hitler.

If he had talked less about India he might have commanded more attention about Germany. His well-justified warnings in the 1930s about German rearmament and British deficiency fell on deaf ears and empty green benches. He occupied his leisure by writing a multi-volume life of his ancestor, the great Duke of Marlborough, and by highly lucrative journalism.

The key question in the 1930s for Britain, France and the Western democracies was how to deal with new powers based on resurgent nationalism – Japan, Italy and Germany. The significant personalities in Britain were Ramsay MacDonald, Stanley Baldwin and Neville Chamberlain in office, and Churchill out of office but impossible to ignore with his wealth of experience and a power of language that put his rivals into the shade. Yet he suffered still from one great handicap – lack of personal trust.

Churchill was slow to recognize the threat of Japan's invasion of China in 1933. Chinese peasants, he thought, might be better off under Japanese rule, and the authority of the League of Nations was scarcely worth invoking. He was equally reluctant to worry about Mussolini, whose regime he supported for its strong hostility to the Bolsheviks and its repression of communism. The rise of Hitler was a different matter. From the outset, Churchill regarded Hitler's regime not only with a deep detestation of its internal nature but also with profound anxiety about its potential menace to Britain. The successive prime ministers in the 1930s did not share his fears. MacDonald was, as Churchill put it, dwindling into senility. Baldwin was satisfied by Hitler's repeated assurances of goodwill towards Britain, and Chamberlain believed that all problems could be solved by diplomacy until too late in the day when it became clear that some could not. Anthony Eden, Foreign Secretary 1935–8, convinced himself that Mussolini was a greater threat than Hitler. The Opposition, led at first by pacifist George Lansbury, cut little political ice and, even when he was replaced by Attlee, who had served in the First World War, it remained divided and confused.

Churchill was the only politician of any stature who regarded Hitler as a serious threat to peace and saw his successive breaches of treaty as a menace to Britain. In fact, Hitler's primary objective was not Britain or France, it was Russia – but if he could only invade Russia safely by first eliminating France and Britain, he would not hesitate to do so. Whatever Hitler's ultimate aims it was clear to Churchill that departure from the League of Nations in 1933, rearmament and conscription in 1935, the occupation of the Rhineland in 1936, the seizure of Austria in 1938, and of the German-speaking region of Czechoslovakia later in the same year, legalized at the Munich Conference, were steps towards a German-dominated Europe that ought to be resisted not by soft-centred diplomacy but by rearmament, especially in the air.

There were many other threats in the 1930s to the worldwide democracy of which Woodrow Wilson dreamed in 1919 – Japan's invasion of China, Mussolini's attack on Abyssinia, the Spanish Civil War. Churchill regarded these as sideshows.

His efforts at persuading the government to greater rearmament were hampered by some of his supporters. Professor Lindemann, his old friend and scientific adviser, was an abrasive figure at daggers drawn with Sir Henry Tizard, a key Establishment member of the world of Whitehall science. There were others in Churchill's entourage who inspired doubts – his son Randolph, Brendan Bracken, Robert Boothby, Duncan Sandys (his son-in-law) and the erratic Beaverbrook. And doubts about Churchill's personal judgement were reinforced by one of his most erratic decisions – to back Edward VIII in his involvement with Mrs Simpson in 1936. He was shouted down in the House and his reputation reached rock-bottom. His friends had implored him to keep quiet but this was something he could seldom do. The apparently ruined career of an elderly, out-of-touch, superannuated politician was saved by the one thing that he wished most to avert – war. The diplomatic revolution that led to Britain's guarantee of Poland owed nothing to Churchill. It stemmed from Hitler's occupation of Prague and the rump Czechoslovakia in March 1939 which gave the lie to the claim that his expansionist policy was simply one of irredentism — restoration of the German-speaking people to their Fatherland. It now seemed limitless and the Nazi-Soviet pact followed by the invasion of Poland confirmed this fear. Britain declared war on 3 September 1939 and France followed suit.

WAR 1939–45

D espite some pressure, Neville Chamberlain had hitherto refused to admit Churchill to the Cabinet. Now he had to. Churchill became First Lord of the Admiralty for the second time, and a member of the War Cabinet. The message 'Winston is back' was flashed to the Fleet. His energy and vitality soon electrified the morale of a Navy that, thanks to apathy and parsimony, had been neglected in the inter-war years. Numerically Britain far outclassed Germany but technologically the German Navy was in many ways superior. There were two spectacular British successes during the winter of 1939 – the battle that forced the pocket battleship *Graf Spee* to sink herself in the River Plate to avoid capture and the rescue of 299 British prisoners from a German prison ship, the *Altmark*, in a

Norwegian fiord. But a heavy blow was sustained when a German submarine penetrated the defences of Scapa Flow and sank the battleship *Ark Royal* with the loss of 833 men.

Churchill's vision was not confined to the Navy. He had strong and controversial views on general strategy, which he put to the Cabinet at what seemed to many members inordinate length. Some of these were fairly eccentric: sowing mines in the Rhine; destroying the Kiel Canal; sending an expeditionary force into the Baltic or alternatively to the far north of Norway in order to interrupt cargoes of iron ore from Sweden to Germany. His most outlandish idea endorsed by other ministers and by the French was to send a force to assist Finland in its war with Russia. Luckily, Finnish resistance came to an end in March 1940 before any troops could be embarked, thus putting paid to 'one of the most bizarre episodes of the war', as Norman Rose puts it.[1]

Churchill followed non-naval events with the keenest interest. Under Professor Lindemann, he established a private statistical section at the Admiralty, whose job was to examine and often criticize the official figures given out by Whitehall. This did not make him popular. But he was always loyal to Chamberlain and, despite past differences, did nothing to undermine the Prime Minister.

In April 1940 Chamberlain agreed to a French plan to mine Norwegian waters but on 9 April Hitler struck first, seizing Denmark and all the major Norwegian ports. The War Cabinet decided to riposte with a counter-invasion, but the Norwegian campaign, for which Churchill took full responsibility, was a disaster of incompetence, confusion and crossed lines from start to finish. It ended with an ignominious withdrawal. People compared it to Gallipoli.

Norway brought down the government. There was a general parliamentary demand for a coalition. Churchill valiantly defended the indefensible but on a vote of confidence Chamberlain's majority fell from 200 to 80. He clearly had to go. Who would succeed? The choice lay between Churchill and the Foreign Secretary, Lord Halifax. The King, Chamberlain and the vast majority of the Conservative Party preferred Halifax. The Labour Party was neutral, determined only not to serve under Chamberlain. However, Halifax was unwilling to take office. And so in this rather circuitous way on 9 May Churchill became Prime Minister.[2] He was far from reluctant: 'All my past life had been but a preparation for this hour and for this trial . . . and I was sure I would not fail', he wrote in his memoirs.[3] Nor did he. His accession to power was one of those few points in history where a single person has altered its course.

For Churchill did something that no one else could have done at that time. With the collapse of France a few weeks later and the intervention of Mussolini on Hitler's side the war had 'objectively' been lost. Europe was at Hitler's feet, all its resources at his command. Although Churchill had even as First Lord courted the evasive, ambiguous and basically anti-British

President Roosevelt, there seemed little hope of rescue from that quarter. If Halifax or any other candidate had become Prime Minister he would almost certainly have accepted a peace settlement on the apparently reasonable terms offered by Hitler via Sweden. Churchill was wrong to say in his memoirs that the question of negotiation was not even considered by the Cabinet. It was, and it was only rejected after much debate. Churchill could not dictate, but he could persuade. Hitler waited in vain for a reply. And having got his way Churchill used his unique power of language both in the Commons and outside, his wonderful gift for public relations, and his indefatigable energy in meeting and talking with people all over the country to convince the British that they had not lost and that somehow or other they would in the end win. At a meeting of ministers he galvanized his audience. 'Every man of you would rise up and tear me down from my place if I were for one moment to contemplate parley or surrender. If this long island story is to end at last, let it end only when each one of us lies choking in his own blood upon the ground'.[4] The decision to reject overtures from Hitler, though later criticized by 'revisionist' historians, was right. It is most unlikely that he would have kept any promise that he made a moment longer than was convenient.

Churchill's great orations were mostly delivered in Parliament and not heard at the time by the public. But one of the most famous was broadcast on 18 June:

> If we fail, then the whole world, including the United States . . . will sink into the abyss of a new Dark Age made more sinister, and perhaps more protracted, by the lights of perverted science. Let us therefore brace ourselves to our duties and so bear ourselves that if the British Empire and its Commonwealth last for a thousand years men will still say, 'This was their finest hour'.[5]

Some of Churchill's rhetoric sounds archaic today and did even back in the 1930s, but the nation's mood had changed by 1940 and the style, which did not change, corresponded to the wartime mood.

On becoming Prime Minister Churchill reconstructed the Cabinet with caution. His political position seemed precarious. He brought in Labour and Liberal figures but the Conservative majority in the House greeted his appointment without enthusiasm. Neville Chamberlain, with a seat in the Cabinet, remained Leader of the Conservative Party – a position to which Churchill was only elected when Chamberlain died in November. By then much had happened. The threat of a German invasion that depended on air dominance had receded after the victory of the RAF Spitfire pilots in the Battle of Britain. As Churchill said, 'Never in the field of human conflict was so much owed by so many to so few'. German bombing of major cities, the misnamed 'Blitz', continued but the worst was over. Churchill was now in undisputed political control. From the beginning he had constituted himself Minister of Defence, an unknown office, as well as Prime Minister. The post gave him undefined power over strategy and over the Chiefs of Staff Committee. He did not abuse it. In the end, however much he bullied them orally and on paper, he never overruled their combined opinion.

Although Churchill had fortified national morale, it was far from clear what strategy Britain should now pursue. The country stood alone against Germany till Hitler invaded Russia in June 1941, and, while Russia struggled for survival, Britain could do little more than hope against hope that 'General Winter' would do to Hitler what it had done to Napoleon in 1812. Few people believed that this would happen. Meanwhile, Churchill made three crucial decisions that shaped British strategy. The first was to prevent the French Navy falling into German hands. This meant attacking and sinking a French battleship and a cruiser at Oran whose commanders refused to accept the British ultimatum. Some 1,200 French sailors were killed and the episode confirmed the bitter hostility of Pétain's Vichy regime.

More important was Churchill's decision to reinforce the British Army in the Middle East and make that the main area for attack on the Axis powers; Italy in particular was the weaker and more vulnerable of the two. Churchill had an obsession with the Mediterranean and this led in the end to the ding-dong battle of the Western Desert, the defeat of German–Italian forces, their expulsion from North Africa and the Anglo-American invasion of Sicily and Italy. In the long run it affected relations with the American Chiefs of Staff and the timing of the Normandy landings in 1944 (Operation Overlord). The strategy was not unanimously agreed. It was one of high risk, and a diversion from the Atlantic U-boat threat, which came so near to knocking Britain out of the war altogether during 1942–3.

A third and even more crucial decision was to make the bombing of German cities the principal means of war against Hitler. The early raids were little more than pinpricks, but by 1944–5 they had escalated into the mass destruction of cities. It was defended as a tit-for-tat for the 'Blitz', as a means of wrecking German war industry. But it was in reality a campaign of terror, one by which Bomber Command, under the ruthless Sir Arthur Harris, provided the only means for an isolated Britain to attack Germany directly. However, there is a contrary view that it diverted resources from more important objectives, particularly the Battle for the Atlantic. Churchill came to have misgivings and the air offensive was singularly ineffective as a means of damaging German war capacity – output actually peaked in the summer of 1944.

Churchill had one great asset that Hitler lacked. This was the brilliant team of crypto-analysts based on Bletchley. The deciphered radio intercepts known as Ultra far outclassed anything achieved in Germany. It was one of the most closely guarded secrets of the war. Churchill had always taken a passionate interest in intelligence. He insisted on seeing not only summaries but also selected items in raw detail too. He called them his 'golden eggs' laid by geese that never cackled. Ultra played a major part in the Battles of Britain and the Atlantic, the Desert War, the Normandy landings and many other theatres of war. Churchill insisted that in the allocation of resources Bletchley should have the highest priority.

The Mediterranean war swung between setbacks and successes. The worst failure was the attempt to prop up Greece, which was invaded by Germany in April 1941. The country was of no strategic value. British forces for the second time were driven into the sea. But for this diversion, the arrival of Rommel and the Afrika Corps in Libya might have been blocked. Rommel inflicted the next serious defeat, the fall of Tobruk in June 1942. Churchill bullied General Auchinleck into defending against his better judgement this so-called 'fortress'. Rommel took 30,000 prisoners and acquired vast dumps of arms and ammunition.

Meanwhile – and many months earlier – America had been drawn into the war. On

7 December 1941 Japan made simultaneous attacks on British and Dutch positions in the Far East. Churchill expected them. What he did not expect was a Japanese attack on the American naval base at Pearl Harbour. He was much relieved, having long feared that Japan would confine her aggression to Britain and Holland, leaving America neutral. 'No American will think it wrong of me', he wrote, 'if I proclaim that to have the United States at our side was to me the greatest joy. . . . So we had won after all! . . . England would live; Britain would live; the Commonwealth of Nations and the Empire would live. . . . Many disasters lay ahead, but there was no more doubt about the end.' A further stroke of luck occurred. Hitler gratuitously declared war on the USA four days after Pearl Harbour, thus enabling Roosevelt to pursue a strategy of 'Germany first'.

As Churchill foresaw, disasters did indeed lie ahead. Japanese forces occupied the whole of Britain's Far East empire, capturing Singapore early in 1942. Rommel very nearly broke through to Cairo in the summer, and Britain survived the Battle of the Atlantic by the narrowest of margins; but the U-boats were defeated in 1943. German forces did not conquer the Middle East. Gibraltar was not attacked. Malta was, but survived. Anglo-American forces drove the Germans out of Libya and Algeria, invaded Italy, whose dictator, Mussolini, was deposed by his king, and engaged in a long and bitter haul up the mountainous peninsula.

Churchill had always wanted 'plenary powers'. He never got them, even when Britain stood alone. He could not ignore the Cabinet and the Chiefs of Staff. After Pearl Harbour he had to face the gradual but inevitable American ascendancy in Allied strategy. The Americans disliked his obsession with the eastern Mediterranean. They wanted an invasion of Europe as soon as possible across the Channel. Churchill rightly resisted a plan to do this in 1942 and managed to divert the Allied armies into clearing North Africa in 1943, which meant postponement of Allied attack in Normandy till

1944. Left to his own devices, Churchill would not have done it even then. But he was now a junior partner in the Allied firm. Despite his hankering after operations in the Balkans or Norway the decision was taken to invade Normandy in June 1944 and it succeeded with far fewer casualties than he had feared. He had little say in the campaigns of 1944–5, which culminated in the surrender of Germany.

Meanwhile, Churchill took an important initiative. At the Moscow Conference in October 1944 he had come to a curious 'percentage' agreement with Stalin about the division of British and Russian post-war interests in the Balkans. The only one that mattered was Greece, where Britain was to have 90 per cent. Stalin soon converted his shares into 100 per cent everywhere else, whatever he had promised. But he kept his word over Greece and did not support the Communists who seemed about to seize the country. Churchill sent troops, and himself spent Christmas 1944 with Eden in Athens. The Communist threat was crushed, to the fury of the Left in Britain and frosty disapproval in America which scented 'colonialism'.

The surrender of Germany on 8 May 1945 had instant political effects in Britain. Churchill wanted the coalition government to continue till the defeat of Japan – a date far from certain. Labour refused; the coalition broke up; Churchill formed a 'caretaker' Cabinet and obtained the dissolution of Parliament on 23 May. The result, which, owing to the delay in counting the Army vote, was not announced till 26 July, was a crushing defeat for the Conservatives by 393 to 213. Churchill, who had been at Potsdam to discuss the peace settlement with Stalin and Truman, promptly resigned. His wife consoled him, saying that his defeat might be a 'blessing in disguise', to which he replied that the disguise was very effective.

Throughout the war years Churchill had been under colossal strain. He had every comfort, as in the past – valets, butlers, cooks, footmen, secretaries, champagne, brandy and cigars. He remained in bed till lunch reading his papers and dictating replies. And he continued to keep an eye on the trivia as well as the major problems. But his ceaseless attendance at summit meetings with Roosevelt and Stalin took their toll on a man who was sixty-five when he became Prime Minister. He was often — and sometimes dangerously — ill. But he had an iron constitution. He survived.

He was irascible, moody, temperamental, rude and insulting. But he had the charm and magic that quickly conjured away resentment. His views on strategy were, are, and always will be a matter of controversy. What is not, is the oratory with which in 1940 he rallied a seemingly defeated nation. Perhaps his worst errors in strategy were his persistence in a Mediterranean policy long after it was necessary, his continued faith in Bomber Command, and his failure to recognize the vulnerability of warships to land-based air attack. Hence the naval disasters off the Malaysian shore in 1941. But these and other quirks are insignificant compared with his main achievement; to make Britain the only power that was in the war at the beginning and survived undefeated until the end.

Churchill's relations with Roosevelt and Stalin have been the subject of much historical debate. He was ostensibly grateful for 'Lend Lease', though he privately regarded it as mortgaging the British Empire. He never admitted recognition of Roosevelt's deep hostility to British 'colonialism', but he must have felt it. Their relationship, under a veneer of candid friendship, was uneasy and their strategic objects divergent. As for Stalin, Churchill with his detestation of 'Bolshevism' had no illusions. He might declare that if Hitler invaded Hell he would say a word for the Devil but their conversations, blurred by copious potations, were mutually mistrustful. Stalin's treatment of Poland and the Warsaw up-rising of 1944 confirmed all Churchill's doubts. But there was little that he could do in dealing with either Stalin or Roosevelt. They had the power. He did not.

CODA 1945–65

Churchill was much distressed at his defeat, which seemed a case of ingratitude only rivalled by King Lear's elder daughters. He had, as he half realized, conducted an inept election campaign. He had taken little interest in domestic affairs. He largely ignored the Beveridge Report, and his claim that Attlee might introduce a modified Gestapo to enforce socialism was rightly regarded as ludicrous. Advised by Lord Beaverbrook, he made error after error in public relations. But the cause of defeat lay deeper. The nation was rejecting not Churchill but the Conservative record since 1931 – slump, failure to rearm, appeasement and sheer longevity in office.

Would Churchill now retire? No; he was determined to win a general election for the first time. But this meant looking five years ahead. He left to others the task of reviving Tory fortunes but he was not going to hand on the torch to Eden until he had to.

He had one great personal consolation in the aftermath of his defeat. Within a short time he found himself very rich. His finances had always been precarious; although he made a large income by his pen in the inter-war years, he had always over-spent it on a style of life that he could not afford. Now, however, the sale of his memoirs of the Second World War produced a huge publishers' advance from the *Daily Telegraph*. Tax accountants and lawyers of the highest level were employed to minimize the demands of the Inland Revenue in a period of punitive taxation of the rich. The *Telegraph* paid £555,000 and there were a host of lucrative spin-offs in America and elsewhere. He never had to worry about money again. He bought land around, and rehabilitated, Chartwell. He bought racehorses. He led the ducal style of life of his forebears.

He was bored by domestic but fascinated by international politics. In 1946 he made his famous 'Iron Curtain' speech at Fulton, Missouri, warning the Western world of the ideological intransigence of the USSR. It went down badly in Britain and none too well in America. Many people still believed in a rapprochement with Stalin. They were wrong and he was right.

Stalin was totally obdurate on all the issues that mattered. The notion, harboured on the left, that socialists could speak to socialists was a myth. Socialism in Britain, however much naïve fellow-travellers deceived themselves, had nothing in common with socialism in the communist version in the USSR. This was soon recognized as clearly by the Attlee government as by its opponents. In the six years before Churchill got back into office in October 1951 the differences between government and opposition on the major issues of foreign policy were relatively trivial. Recognition of the Cold War and the importance of Anglo-

American cooperation was common to both sides. On the Conservative right and the Labour left for different reasons there was mistrust of America but this was never more than a dissident minority opinion which cut little ice.

The real problem that faced post-war Britain was economic but this was not a field in which Churchill excelled or took any great interest – at any rate when he was in opposition. In government he had to give it some attention but even then he left it largely to others. On the international scene he was undoubtedly the most famous and conspicuous figure in the world. His personal prestige was immense. Whenever he spoke he dominated the headlines, not always with universal assent, for example the Fulton speech, but certainly with universal attention.

There were two major problems, apart from the Cold War, which worried him in the immediate post-war years. One was Palestine. He believed in a Jewish state but his ardour cooled in 1944 after the murder in Cairo of Lord Moyne, a lifelong friend, by Jewish terrorists. However, in 1948 when Israel had become a *fait accompli* he supported recognition in a series of speeches. The other problem was India. Given his past record in the 1930s Churchill could hardly be expected to be keen on Indian self-government. But in 1942 his Cabinet had gone far towards pledging ultimate partition into separate Hindu and Muslim states with the right to independence. He believed that there was a grave risk of civil commotion and bloodshed if this process were undertaken too soon, and the events which followed in 1947 seemed to bear out this prophecy. What he would have done had he still been in office must be a matter of guesswork. Perhaps he was not entirely sorry that the responsibility lay elsewhere. It is pleasant to know that after many years of fierce denunciation he made it up with Nehru in the end and accepted as inevitable the independence of India and Pakistan.

On another question – of great controversy

today – Churchill has been misunderstood. In opposition he often spoke of the importance of European unity. At Zurich University in September 1946 he made a speech which attracted notable publicity but gave rise to retrospective misunderstanding. Concerned with the reconstruction of post-war Europe he boldly suggested, amid much surprise, that France and Germany should reconcile the differences that had caused them to fight each other three times in the previous eighty years. What was needed, he said, was a new 'European family', 'a kind of United States of Europe'. Britain should make every effort to bring this about but could not be a part of it. Britain, the Commonwealth and 'mighty America', together with, he hoped, the Soviet Union would act as friends and sponsors of the new Europe of his vision and 'champion its right to live and shine'.[1]

It is a myth, though often repeated, that Churchill was in favour of joining a federal Europe, if that is what he meant by a 'United

States of Europe'. But Churchill was a British nationalist. The idea of Britain having the sort of relationship with a European federal capital which Texas or California has with Washington was never in his mind. When he got back into office in 1951 he soon stopped talking about Europe and, supported by Eden, took the same line as Attlee had towards British participation in the Schuman Plan, the Coal and Steel Community which was the ancestor of the European Union.[2] To the chagrin of Euro-enthusiasts he refused to join it.

The Fulton and Zurich speeches, whether or not by intention, may have contributed to the more positive part soon played by the USA in European affairs, exemplified by the Truman Doctrine and the Marshall Plan promulgated in March and June 1947 respectively. Churchill strongly supported these developments. In Norman Rose's words he 'stormed Western public opinion and captured it on behalf of the Cold War. It was a task eminently suited to his unique talents'.[3] In 1949 the North Atlantic

Treaty was signed in Washington with his strong approval.

In his opposition years he was far less active on the home front than on the international scene. The paramount need for the leader of a Conservative party defeated by the largest margin since 1906 was to reconstruct its organization and make it fit to face the next general election. In the event this was achieved.

By the time the next general election was becoming imminent (late 1949) the Conservatives were far better placed to fight it than they had been in 1945. But the recovery owed little to Churchill personally apart from his name which still held a magic for the rank and file of the party whatever the misgivings of the grandees. Their doubts had mounted since the Fulton Speech. There can be no question that an influential group would have liked his retirement and replacement by Eden. Clementine Churchill herself had hoped that he would bow out after the electoral débâcle if not at once, at least within a year, and devote himself to his memoirs instead of politics. Churchill had every intention of doing both, though perhaps 'devote' is the wrong word for his attitude to politics. His frequent travels and long absences from Parliament were the subject of private adverse comment.

Meanwhile his senior colleagues spent much time and thought on reconstructing the party machine. Lord Woolton and Rab Butler were key figures in this operation helped by a group of bright younger men who had served in the war. Churchill had little use for those who had not, and even if they had he was sceptical about some of their new policies and initiatives being adumbrated in the form of various 'charters' which were somewhat to the left by Tory standards. Of their authors he said on one occasion, 'They are no more than a set of pink pansies'. In any case he believed that the job of the Opposition was to oppose government policies, not set out detailed alternatives which might create hostages to fortune. He did not obstruct the activities of Woolton, Butler and their acolytes but he viewed them without enthusiasm, and took little part himself.

The post-war years of opposition saw him in a bad mood. He missed the red boxes, the feeling of being 'in the know', and the power to take decisions which affected events. His large income cushioned him to some extent against the bleak austerities of rationing; he was never short of cigars, champagne and brandy. But England was a dismal place for many years after the war. No wonder he went abroad as often as he could to stay at Lord Beaverbrook's villa in the South of France or at the even more splendid house of his Hungarian-born literary agent Emery Reves who had made a fortune both for Churchill and himself.

His relations with his family were strained. Clementine had always had to put up with his black moods and his enigmatic unpredictability but she was finding it more difficult to cope as the years went by. There were continual rows and she seldom accompanied him on foreign visits. There was much family trouble — broken marriages, alcoholism, mental depression. He had an uneasy relationship with Randolph and with his two elder daughters, Sarah and Diana. The fixed point in these turbulent family waters was his youngest daughter Mary who was devoted, calm and reliable. In 1947 she married Christopher Soames. It was a notably stable and successful marriage. His son-in-law was to be a pillar of strength to Churchill in his old age.

During these post-war years he had the consolation of considerable success in writing his memoirs. Planned as five volumes they came out in six, the first in 1948, the last in 1954 and they made a great deal of money (see p. 86). He was helped by a large and able team of collaborators but they were in no sense ghost writers. Every word was his own.

By the beginning of 1950 Labour's fortunes were palpably in decline. The public was fed up with austerity, rationing and bureaucratic controls. In 1949 Attlee tried to modify these wartime legacies but it was too late to make much impression. The election of February

1950 reduced his overall majority to six.
Eighteen months later the Conservatives won a
Commons overall majority of seventeen,
although with fewer votes than Labour from the
electorate.

Churchill at the age of nearly seventy-seven
thus became Prime Minister for the third time.
He was tired and increasingly deaf. He had
survived three bouts of pneumonia and in 1949
while staying with Beaverbrook he had had a
minor stroke. During the 1950 election
campaign he suffered what his physician, Lord
Moran called a 'spasm of the cerebral arteries'.
Noting in his diary, Moran said, 'This is the
beginning of trouble . . . there can be only one
end to it. How long it will last is only
guesswork'.[4] But Churchill had no intention of
quitting the stage on which he had figured for
half a century.

The 1951 election had been more
acrimonious than usual. Labour charged
Churchill with being a warmonger – hence the
notorious slogan 'Whose finger on the trigger?'

And it was also claimed that the Conservatives would dismantle the welfare state and confront the trade unions. These allegations which he strongly repudiated conditioned much of Churchill's policy. In practice, whatever his rhetoric, he was a conciliator who had always hankered after a coalition government transcending party politics. This was something which he had favoured even before 1914 and in which he took his part from 1917 to 1922 and from 1940 to 1945. A coalition was not viable in 1951 but he could do the next best thing and temper a Tory Cabinet with eminent non-political figures whom he knew from his wartime premiership. Thus Lord Ismay, Lord Leathers, Sir Walter Monckton (a very luke-warm Tory), Lord Alexander of Tunis and Churchill's old friend Lord Cherwell (who certainly held right-wing views but had never been trusted by the Conservative hierarchy) entered the Cabinet. The key posts went to Eden as Foreign Secretary, Rab Butler as Chancellor of the Exchequer and Harold

Macmillan as Minister of Housing with the task of building the 300,000 houses promised in the election manifesto. But an effort to have a small group of 'super-ministers' came to nothing. Whitehall as usual prevailed.

Predictably Churchill's main interest was in foreign and defence policy. The Korean war had already begun and he supported the Labour government's policy of a limited contribution to the campaign. He had been very critical of Herbert Morrison's handling of the oil crisis in Iran and was pleased by the CIA's successful plot to reinstate the Shah. He reluctantly accepted British withdrawal from Egypt. But above all else in foreign policy he sought a revival of the 'special relationship' with Washington and, after Stalin's death in 1953, a summit meeting between himself and the new leaders of the USA and the USSR to deal with the terrifying possibilities of the nuclear bomb. Nothing came of these overtures but the possibility was an excuse for staying on as Prime Minister in, as he thought, a unique position to broker such a deal.

Half-American though he was, Churchill mistook the invariable courtesy of Eisenhower for a closer political rapport than actually existed.

Eisenhower knew the realities of power. When in July 1954 Churchill sent a message to Moscow, without consulting either the President or his own Cabinet, suggesting a bilateral 'friendly Meeting with no Agenda', he was rebuffed by both Malenkov and Eisenhower. From then onwards the pressure from colleagues for his resignation was never relaxed.

Churchill did nothing notable in the field of defence after returning to power in 1951. For a few months he combined the two offices of Minister of Defence and Prime Minister as in wartime but soon desisted. He left economic policy to Butler, though on Lord Cherwell's advice he did stamp on the Chancellor's plan called 'Robot' to make sterling convertible in 1952. The most criticized aspect of his home policy was his treatment of the trade unions. He appointed Sir Walter Monckton, an 'all things to all people' appeaser, as Minister of Labour. Churchill at this time was terrified of the unions for a host of past personal and political reasons. Some of his colleagues were uneasy but the unions were led by seemingly 'responsible' chiefs unlike the militant figures who nearly destroyed the economy twenty-five years later. If Churchill and Monckton gave too much ground, the consequences were not apparent till long after.

There was much private unease in the party elite about Churchill's continuance in office. He was not 'ga-ga' as alleged. His mind was clear, he could make commanding speeches in the House, answer questions and floor his opponents. He did not drink any more than he always had and the effects were no greater. But with age he tired more easily, grew more deaf and became more garrulous in Cabinet where it was difficult for colleagues to get in a word. In June 1953 he had a serious stroke which was effectively concealed from the media in a way impossible today. But he made an amazing recovery and addressed the party conference in October with a speech which electrified his loyal audience. He ought to have retired in 1953 but his excuse was Eden's simultaneous illness and the problem of succession. By now there were many people who thought it was time for him to go but he hated to give up the power which was the breath of his existence, the adrenalin which kept him going. The problem was who should bell the cat, and there was much reluctance to take the initiative. In the end Macmillan did and after several changes of mind Churchill agreed to resign in April 1955. He was already loaded with honours – the Order of Merit, the Garter, the Nobel Prize for Literature ('£12,000 free of tax – not so bad,' he told Clementine). The Queen offered him a dukedom; told in advance that he would almost certainly refuse, she was much relieved that he actually did. But one honour that Churchill received gave him anything but pleasure. For his eightieth birthday in 1954 the House of Commons subscribed to present him with a portrait by Graham Sutherland. He detested it, rightly if one judges by photographs, and they are the only source since Clementine knowing his distress secretly destroyed the original a few years later.

Churchill's inevitable successor was Anthony Eden. Despite his increasing doubts about the calibre of the 'crown prince' Churchill did not, indeed could not, do anything to stop him. And he cannot have faulted Eden's first important political decision – to hold an election as soon as possible which he won by fifty-eight seats, a comfortable increase in the Conservative majority.

Churchill's Indian Summer, as Anthony Seldon entitled his study of the old statesman's last premiership, has been too often dismissed as the dim twilight of a great career. It was in reality one of the most successful and least crisis-ridden of all post-war administrations. The dire predictions of Labour spokesmen during the 1951 election campaign were wildly misplaced. There was no sabre-rattling and no 'gung-ho' imperialism. There was no attempt to dismantle the welfare state or to confront organized labour. The promised 300,000 houses were actually built even sooner than expected, despite Treasury objections which Churchill overruled. It was a conciliatory middle-of-the-road government which gave the electorate what it wanted after the stresses of war and the strains of reconstruction – peace, prosperity, quiet and a steadily rising standard of living.

Churchill was to live for another nine years after a retirement which he resented but must have known to be inevitable. He was depressed and lethargic at first but found a new interest in horse-racing which he could now afford and an old interest in completing his *History of the English Speaking Peoples* which he had laid aside since the 1930s for the duration of a political career which only ended in 1955. The final volume of his *War Memoirs* had come out a year before his retirement. They will always remain an important historical source as long as the reader remembers that they are essentially a defence of his wartime record, his 'case'. written while many people were alive whom it was inexpedient to offend. They need a critical assessment in the light of the mass of information which has been available subsequently.

The four volumes of his *History of the English Speaking Peoples* (1956–58) are, like everything he wrote, wonderfully readable. But they are a lop-sided version of history reflecting his own interests – war and politics – and do not contain much about social and economic matters or the history of ideas. However, one cannot have everything and historians are themselves a product of their time and place and personality. The volumes are quintessentially Churchillian.

After a melancholy twilight in which he became increasingly deaf and infirm he died on 24 January 1965. A multiplicity of tributes were paid to him. The leading figures of the world attended a state funeral on 30 January in St Paul's Cathedral on a scale of grandeur unequalled since that of the Duke of Wellington. Churchill was finally laid to rest in the churchyard of Bladon near Blenheim Palace where he had been born.

NOTES

CHAPTER ONE

1. Winston S. Churchill, *My Early Life* (London, Fontana Books, 1959), p. 53.
2. Ibid., p. 54.
3. Ibid., p. 91.
4. Ibid., pp. 96–7.
5. Randolph S. Churchill, *Winston S. Churchill*, Vol. I, *Youth 1874–1900* (London, Heinemann, 1966), p. 288.
6. Winston S. Churchill, *op. cit.*, pp. 107–8.
7. Ibid., p. 121.
8. Ibid., p. 122.

CHAPTER TWO

1. Randolph S. Churchill, *op. cit.*, p. 251.
2. Winston S. Churchill, *op. cit.*, p. 372. Italics as in original text.

CHAPTER FOUR

1. Quoted Henry Pelling, *Winston Churchill* (London, Macmillan, 1974), p. 229.

CHAPTER FIVE

1. Norman Rose, *Churchill, An Unruly Life* (London, Simon and Schuster, 1994), p. 259.
2. Robert Blake and Wm. Roger Louis (eds), *Churchill* (Oxford, Oxford University Press, 1993), chapter 15 by Robert Blake.

3. Winston S. Churchill, *The Second World War* (London, Cassell, 1948), Vol. 1, pp. 526–7.
4. Quoted Rose, *op. cit.*, pp. 264–5.
5. Quoted ibid., p. 268.

CHAPTER SIX

1. Rose, *op. cit.*, p. 332.
2. The best analyis of Churchill's attitude to Europe is by Lord Beloff in Blake and Louis, *op. cit.*, chapter 25.
3. Rose, *op. cit.*, p. 333.
4. Lord Moran, *Winston Churchill, The Struggle for Survival 1940–55* (London, Constable, 1966), pp. 357–60.

BIBLIOGRAPHY

Addison, Paul. *Churchill on the Home Front*, London, Cape, 1992

Ashley, Maurice. *Churchill as Historian*, London, Secker & Warburg, 1968

Blake, Robert, and Louis, Wm. Roger (eds). *Churchill*, Oxford, Oxford University Press, 1993

Bonham-Carter, Violet. *Winston Churchill as I Knew Him*, London, Eyre and Spottiswoode, 1965

Brown, Anthony Montague. *Long Sunset*, London, Cassell, 1995

Charmley, John. *Churchill, The End of Glory*, London, Hodder, 1993

Churchill, Winston S. *Great Contemporaries*, London, Butterworth, 1937

——. *The World Crisis 1911–18*, London, Odhams, 2 vols, 1938

——. *The Second World War*, London, Cassell, 6 vols, 1948–54

——. *My Early Life: A Roving Commission*, London, Fontana, 1959

The Collected Essays of Sir Winston Churchill, London, Library of Imperial History, 1976

Colville, John. *Footprints in Time*, London, Collins, 1976

Cosgrave, Patrick. *Churchill at War, Alone 1939–40*, London, Collins, 1974

Gilbert, Martin. *Churchill, A Life*, London, Heineman, 1991

Jablonsky, David. *Churchill, the Great Game and Total War*, London, Cass, 1991

Bibliography

James, Robert Rhodes. *Churchill: A Study in Failure 1900–1939*, London, Weidenfeld & Nicolson, 1970

Lamb, Richard. *Churchill as War Leader, Right or Wrong*, London, Bloomsbury, 1991

Lewin, Ronald. *Churchill as Warlord*, London, Batsford, 1973

Moran, Lord. *Winston Churchill, The Struggle for Survival 1940–55*, London, Constable, 1966

Parker, Robert. *Winston Churchill: Studies in Statesmanship*, London, Brassey's (UK), 1995

Pelling, Henry. *Winston Churchill*, London, Macmillan, 1974

Roberts, Andrew. *Eminent Churchillians*, London, Phoenix, 1994

Rose, Norman. *Churchill: An Unruly Life*, London, Simon & Schuster, 1994

Soames, Mary. *Clementine Churchill*, London, Cassell, 1979

Wheeler-Bennett, John, *et al*. *Action This Day: Working with Churchill*, London, Macmillan, 1968

POCKET BIOGRAPHIES

FORTHCOMING

W.G. Grace
Donald Trelford

The Brontës
Kathryn White

Lawrence of Arabia
Jeremy Wilson

Christopher Columbus
Peter Rivière

Martin Luther King
Harry Harmer

POCKET BIOGRAPHIES

AVAILABLE

David Livingstone
C.S. Nicholls

Margot Fonteyn
Alistair Macaulay

Winston Churchill
Robert Blake

Abraham Lincoln
H.G. Pitt

Charles Dickens
Catherine Peters

Enid Blyton
George Greenfield

George IV
Michael De-la-Noy

Christopher Wren
James Chambers

Che Guevara
Andrew Sinclair

Beethoven
Anne Pimlott Baker

POCKET BIOGRAPHIES

Scott of the Antarctic
Michael De-la-Noy

Alexander the Great
E.E. Rice

Sigmund Freud
Stephen Wilson

Marilyn Monroe
Sheridan Morley and
Ruth Leon

Rasputin
Harold Shukman

Jane Austen
Helen Lefroy

Mao Zedong
Delia Davin

Marie and Pierre Curie
John Senior

Ellen Terry
Moira Shearer

For a copy of our complete list or details of other Sutton titles, please contact Regina Schinner at Sutton Publishing Limited, Phoenix Mill, Thrupp, Stroud, Gloucestershire, GL5 2BU